I0147267

Charles Chauncy

A letter to a friend:

Containing remarks on certain passages in a sermon preached by the Right

Reverend Father in God, John Lord Bishop of Landaff, before the

Incorporated Society for the Propagation of the Gospel in Foreign Parts, at

their annivers

Charles Chauncy

A letter to a friend:
Containing remarks on certain passages in a sermon preached by the Right Reverend Father in God, John Lord Bishop of Landaff, before the Incorporated Society for the Propagation of the Gospel in Foreign Parts, at their annivers

ISBN/EAN: 9783337713898

Printed in Europe, USA, Canada, Australia, Japan

Cover: Foto ©ninafisch / pixelio.de

More available books at **www.hansebooks.com**

Dr. *Chauncy*'s

REMARKS

On certain PASSAGES in

The Biſhop of LANDAFF's

SOCIETY-SERMON,

A

LETTER
To a FRIEND,

CONTAINING,

REMARKS on certain PASSAGES in a

SERMON

Preached, by the Right Reverend Father
in GOD, *John Lord Bishop of Landaff*,
before the Incorporated Society for the
Propagation of the Gospel in Foreign
Parts, at their Anniversary Meeting in the
Parish Church of St. *Mary-Le-Bow*, *Fe-
bruary* 20. 1767. In which the highest
Reproach is undeservedly cast upon the
AMERICAN COLONIES.

By CHARLES CHAUNCY, D. D.
Pastor of the first Church of Christ in *Boston*.

BOSTON: Printed by KNEELAND and ADAMS
in Milk-Street, for THOMAS LEVERETT, in Corn-hill.
MDCCLXVII.

S I R,

THIS waits upon you with my thanks for
  sending me the Lord Bishop of Landaff's
  sermon, preached last February before the
Society for the propagation of the Gospel in
foreign parts ; though I am sorry it was accom-
panied with your desire, after I had carefully read
it, to give you my thoughts concerning those paffages in it which relate to the American Colonies.
You could not have selected a person better fit-
ted to answer your design, so far as a warm
affection for this as well as the Mother-Country,
and a strong attachment to the interest and honor
of both, may be esteemed requisite qualifications ;
but you might, in regard of leisure and abilities,
with much more propriety, have enjoined this
fervice on some others of your acquaintance :
However, my obligations to you are such, that
I could not excuse my self from attempting that,
which, I join with you in thinking, justice to the
Colonies requires should be done upon this occasion.

Had

Had the character you mention, as given the British Colonies, been contained in a discourse delivered by a common Clergy-man, before a common audience, it would, I believe, have given you no uneasiness; as you would not have been apprehensive of any harm from it: But, as it is exhibited in a sermon, preached before the incorporated Society for the propagation of the Gospel in foreign parts, many of whom are high in rank, and sustain the greatest character, no wonder your concern was moved; especially, as this respectable body of men have virtually made themselves patrons of the sermon. So we are authorised to think from their voting the preacher thanks for it, and desiring him to deliver to them a copy of it for the press; unless it may be said, this was only a matter of form and ceremony; to suppose which would reflect dishonor on its dignified author. We, in this part of the world, must be shamefully impious and immoral, to deserve what is here said of us; or, if we do not, very unhappy to be publickly placed in so injurious a point of light. Whether we are the one, or the other, I shall now examine.

His Lordship says, Pag. 6. " Since the discovery of the new world, the same provision hath not been made of ministers, necessary to the support of Christianity among those who removed thither; especially in the British Colonies". If
the

the complaint here made, fo far as the Colonies
without difcrimination are concerned in it, lies in
this, that they have not provided themfelves with
minifters *epifcopally ordained*, they readily own
the fact. But, furely, his Lordfhip does not
think, that fuch minifters are *fo neceffary* that
Chriftianity cannot be fupported without them.
This doctrine was taught, and believed, in
former times, when bigotry and oppreffion were
the characteriftic of fome that were placed in
high offices both in church and ftate ; but, in
the prefent day of enlarged knowledge and freedom of inquiry, it is hoped there is no Arch-
Bifhop, or Bifhop in England, of fuch contracted
principles. Certainly, his Lordfhip is more catholic in his fentiments : Otherwife He might
have been more extenfive in his complaint, by taking in Scotland, Holland, and many of the reform-
ed proteftant churches in Europe ; for they, as
truly as the Britifh Colonies in America, are not
provided with minifters "neceffary to the fupport
of Chriftianity" among them, if Epifcopal ones
only are fufficient for the purpofe. It is therefore
probable, the meaning of the charge againft the
Colonies is, that they had provided themfelves
with no minifters at all, or had been fo fcanty in
their provifion, that Chriftianity, on this account, muft fink and die, having no better a fupport. But this, affirmed of the Colonies without diftinction, or limitation, is fo contrary to the

truth

truth of fact, and might have so easily been known to be so, that I cannot but wonder at his Lordship's charge. It can, with honor to him, be in no way accounted for but by supposing, that he was some how or other strangely misinformed. Blessed be God, we in New-England, now have, and all along from the first settlement of the Country have had, a full provision of Gospel-ministers. * Had they been consecrated after the mode of the established Church at home, and his Lordship had known their number and just character, he would, I doubt not, have reversed what he has here said, and have spoken largely in commendation of, at least, these parts of the American world.

The

* Within the limits of New-England, there are now, at the lowest computation, not less than five hundred and fifty ministers, some Presbyterian, mostly Congregational, who have been regularly separated to the pastoral charge of as many christian societies; having been first educated, and graduated, at one or other of our colleges. They may be justly farther characterised as men of a good moral conversation. For so sacred a regard is paid here to the apostle Paul's directions to Timothy and Tius, that a minister is surely dismissed from his office, if it appears, that he is not " blameless as a steward of God, sober, holy, just and temperate in all things." It has been said by strangers who have come among us, and by some Church-Clergymen too, that the work of the ministry is not more faithfully and diligently performed in any part of the christian world.

The fermon goes on, pag. ibid. " A fcandalous negiect, (this of not making a provifion of
minifters) which hath brought great and deferved reproach both on the adventurers, and on the
goverment whence they went ; and under whofe
protection and power they ftill remained in their
new habitations". How far the government at
home have brought upon themfelves " deferved
reproach" for this " fcandalous neglect", I prefume not to fay ; but this I will venture to fay,
that they were as deficient in " protecting" the
adventurers, as in " providing minifters" for
them. It is well known here, if not in England,
that it was from themfelves, without any affiftance from the government whence they came,
that they founded and fettled th.s new world,
amidft a thoufand hardfhips, and in oppofition
to the furious malice of the Indian favages, with
whom they were at war, at one time and another, at a vaft expence of blood and treafure, as
long as they lived ; and their pofterity after
them were many years expofed to like difficulties
and dangers, and went chearfully through them
without help afforded to them from the native
home of their fathers.

His Lordfhip proceeds, pag. ibid. " To the
" adventurers, what reproach could be caft, hea-
" vier than they deferved ? Who, with their
" native foil, abandoned their native manners and

" religion ;

" religion ; and e'er long were found in many
" parts living without remembrance or knowledge
" of God, without any Divine worſhip, in diſſolute
" wickedneſs, and the moſt brutal profligacy of
" manners. Inſtead of civiliſing and converting
" barbarous infidels, as they undertook to do,
" they became themſelves infidels and barbari-
" ans. And is it not ſome aggravation of their
" ſhame, that this their neglect of religion was
" contrary to the pretences and conditions under
" which they obtained Royal grants, and public
" authority to their adventures ? The pretences
" and conditions were, that their deſign was, and
" that they ſhould endeavour, the enlargement
" of Commerce, and the propagation of chriſti-
" an faith. The former they executed with
" ſincerity and zeal ; and in the latter moſt no-
" torioully failed". A ſtranger to the hiſtory
of theſe adventurers would be obviouſly and
unavoidably led, from the deſcription in this
paragraph, to conceive of them, " in many
parts" at leaſt, as impious, profligate and diſſo-
lutely wicked to the higheſt degree of guilt. A
blacker character could not have been given of
them.

But, in " what parts" were the adventurers
thus loſt to all ſenſe of God and religion ? His
Lordſhip has not told us in direct terms ; but
he has ſo clearly and fully pointed out the ad-

venturers

venturers he had in view, by certain defcriptive marks, that we can be at no lofs to know his meaning in the limiting words, " many parts " Such are thefe that follow, " their not civilifing and converting the barbarous infidels, as they UNDERTOOK TO DO" ; their neglect of this inftance of religion " in contrariety to the PRETENCES and CONDITIONS under which they obtained ROYAL GRANTS" ; and, finally, thefe pretences and conditions declaring, that " their DESIGN WAS, and that THEY WOULD ENDEAVOUR, THE PROPAGATION OF THE CHRISTIAN FAITH". There were no adventurers to America, who undertook to convert the native barbarians, and to whom Royal grants were made upon this condition, unlefs it were thofe who came into New-England. Thefe therefore muft be the adventurers his Lordfhip had more efpecially in his eye.

And of thefe he declares, " that, with their native foil, they abandoned their native manners and religion". His Lordfhip could not affirm this from perfonal knowledge, as thefe adventurers were all dead long before he came into being. And it is difficult to fay whence he could collect fo aftonifhing an account. It is not contained in any hiftory that was ever wrote, either of them, or of the fettlement of the Country by them. No Miffionary from the Society, it is candidly believed, could be fo bafely wicked, as

to tranfmit it home, it is fo flanderous and falfe ;
Nor can it eafily be conceived how his Lordfhip could come by it, unlefs from fome one, or
more, who, being difaffected to the Colonies,
and malicioufly fet againft them, took an un-
bounded liberty in fpeaking evil of them, even
from their firft beginnings. Thefe adventurers
have fometimes been blamed for having too much
religion ; but never before, within my knowledge,
for having none, or for having loft what they
had in their " native" land.

It is acknowledged, if their "native religion" lay
in a blind fubmiffion to Church-power, arbitrarily
exercifed, they did " abandon" it ; and their
virtue hereby difcovered will be fpoken of to
their honor, throughout all generations, by thofe
acquainted with it, who really believe, in its juft
latitude, this undoubted Gofpel-truth, namely,
that Jefus Chrift only is fupreme Head and Lord
of the chriftian Church.

But if by " abandoning their native religion"
is meant, their renouncing the doctrines of Chriftianity as held forth in the thirty nine articles of
the Church of England, the reverfe of what is
here faid is the truth. Thefe indeed are the
doctrines that were handed down from them to
their children and children's children ; infomuch
that they are to this day the ftandard of ortho-
doxy ; and there are comparatively few but are

orthodox

orthodox in this fenfe, unlefs among thofe who profefs themfelves members of the Epifcopal Churches. Or if by " abandoning their native religion" the thing intended is, " that e'er long they were found without remembrance, or knowledge of God, or any divine worfhip", as the charge againft them goes on in the next words ; it muft be plainly faid, it is altogether groundlefs. There is no fact relative to the Country more certain, than that thefe adventurers fo far " remembred and knew God", as to make it one of their firft cares to provide for the carrying on, maintaining and upholding the worfhip of him, which they did wherever they extended their fettlements ; and their pofterity have conftantly took the like care all along to the prefent day. There is therefore no fenfe in which the above reprefentation can comport with truth but this, that God cannot be worfhipped, at leaft fo as that it may be proper to fay he is, unlefs the worfhip be carried on according to the manner of the eftablifhed Englifh Church. Some of the Society's Miffionaries, I have reafon to believe, are much inclined to think thus ; but I would not fupect fuch a thing of his Lordfhip. What he has here faid I would rather attribute to mifinformation.

It feems to be allowed, that thefe adventurers had " native manners" ; otherwife they could not, upon leaving their " native foil, " abandon them ;

them". But, they muſt have abandoned them
to an enormous height of guilt, to juſtifie their
being charged " with diſſolute wickedneſs, and
the moſt brutal profligacy of mann rs". Theſe
words are ſo groſly reproachful, that I could
ſcarce believe my own eyes, when I ſaw them
in his Lordſhip's ſermon. He muſt certainly,
however inſenſible of it, have correſponded, by
word, or writing, with ſome vile Calumniator.

It would be injuſtice to the firſt fathers of
New-England, if I did not ſay upon this occaſion,
that ſome of them were exceeded by few, in
point of natural, or acquired accompliſhments ;
and by far the greater part of them were emi-
nently holy men ; pious toward God, jealous of
the honor of Chriſt as ſole head of the Church,
ſober, juſt, kind, meek, patient, diſengaged in
their affection to things on the earth, and intirely
reſigned to the alwiſe righteous Governor of the
univerſe. And of this they exhibited the ſtrong-
eſt evidence by their truly chriſtian deportment
under far greater tryals than good men are ordinarily called to. They forſook every thing near
and dear to them in their native land, from a
regard to him who is " King in Sion". And
when they removed to the then American wilds,
and found themſelves ſeparated from their friends
by a wide Ocean, without the conveniences, and
often in want even of the neceſſaries of life, ſur-
rounded with difficulties, and expoſed to all
manner

manner of hardships and dangers, what could tempt them to continue here, if they had been those " infidels, barbarians, diffolutely wicked and brutal profligates", they are reprefented by his Lordfhip to have been ? What, in this cafe, could have prevented their return to their friends, and the comforts of their native home ? As they are fuppofed to have loft all confcience towards God, if they ever had any, Church impofitions could have been no obftacle in their way. They might, in fhort, with infinitely more reafon, have been fpoken of as fools, or mad-men, than irreligious profligates. It may, I believe, be faid with ftrict truth, there are none, now in England, of any denomination, in high or low office, or none at all, who are under circumftances that put it in their power to give fuch indubitable proof of their being truly upright good men. And I wifh they may never fee the time when they will have opportunity, by fimilar tryals, to give as good evidence of their integrity. The Miffionaries from the Society at home may be efteemed there men of uncommon attainments in Chriftian piety, difcovered in their zeal to promote the caufe of Chrift ; but they never yet exhibited, and, in all probability, will never be able to exhibit, like ample proof that this is their real character. No Miffionary was ever fent hither, till the Country, through a vaft extent, was fubdued, cultivated and fettled, fo

as

as to render living here comfortable and pleaâ
fant. And as they are moftly fixed in populous towns, in which they may eafily be fur-
nifhed with conveniences, and are expofed to
no hardfhips or hazards but what are common
to mankind in general ; they can have opportunity to give no other than common evidence
of the goodnefs of their charaĉter ; and while
they give this, we will own ourfelves fatisfied
with it, though others fhould not be fatisfied
with that which is much ftronger, in regard
of much more important men.

I fhall only add here, The adventurers to
this then inhofpitable land, muft have the
honor of being owned the original fettlers of a
Country, which, in time, if not prevented by
oppreffive meafures, will probably enlarge the
Britifh Empire in extent, grandeur, riches and
power, far beyond what has ever yet been
known in the world. It is pity, after fuch a
long courfe of labors, hardfhips, dangers and
fufferings, as they heroicly went through, to
prepare the way to what the Country now is,
and may be in after times ; I fay, it is pity
their afhes fhould be raked into, and their
memory treated with reproach, greater than
which was never deferved by any of the fons
of Adam, in any part of the earth. They
are gone to receive the reward of their fidelity
to their Savior and Lord ; and their reward, it

may

may be, will be inhanced by means of the un-
deferved obloquies that have been caft upon
them in this fermon.

As to the charge, in the next words, that,
" inftead of civilifing and converting barbarous infidels, as they undertook to do, they
became themfelves infidels and barbarians" ;
and that it was " fome aggravation of their
fhame, that this their neglect of religion was
contrary to the pretences and conditions, under
which they obtained Royal grants, and public
authority to their adventures" : As to this
charge, I fay, it would, I believe, if faftened
upon any other body of men, profeffing godli-
nefs, be efteemed highly unchriftian. Had a
hint only of this nature been fuggefted, relative to the Society in whofe audience this
cenfure was delivered, this, and much worfe,
would have been faid of it, and defervedly too.
And yet, that Society have, without all doubt,
been as deficient in their endeavours to propagate the Gofpel in thefe " foreign parts",
where it was moft needed, and in contrariety
to the defign of their incorporation too, as was
ever true of thefe adventurers. * For, by far

C   the

* What has been done by thefe adventurers may be
feen in the general account that is given of their
labors in fome following notes. And if the facts
there related fhould be fet in contraft with the
abftracts of the Society, relative to the Indians, it
will

the greater part of their money has been expended, if we may judge by their own abſtracts, not in miſſions to convert the Indian-
natives, not in miſſions to ſet up and maintain
the

will appear at once, that, from the time of their
incorporation to this day, they have done little,
very little, in compariſon therewith. Their principal care has been to propagate the church of
England ; and this, not ſo much in thoſe places,
where there was real need of Miſſionaries for the
inſtruction of people in the knowledge of Chriſt,
or to ſet up the worſhip of God among them, as
where there was a fullneſs of means for ſuch inſtruction, and divine worſhip was already ſet up,
and as generally and devoutly attended as in England it ſelf. Many thouſands of pounds ſterling
have been thus expended, where there was no want
of it for the propagation of the Goſpel, unleſs that
means the propagation of the Epiſcopal mode of
ſerving God. And what has been the effect of
this vaſt expence ? If we look over the Society's
abſtracts, we ſhall find one account from their
Miſſionaries is, " We have baptiſed ſo many within ſuch a time ; ſo many adult, and ſo many children, white or black" : Every one of which might
as well have been baptiſed without a ſhilling of
this expence, if it might have been done by miniſters not *epiſcopally* qualified for this work. Another
account amounts to this, " There is the proſpect
of a Church in this and the other place ; we have
been invited to preach here and there ; ſo many
have profeſſed themſelves members of the Church,
and more are inclined this way". But of whom are
theſe declarations made ? Not of thoſe, who were
brought up in ignorance of the chriſtian religion ;
not of thoſe, who were deſtitute of the means of
ſalvation ; not of thoſe, who had not the opportunity, and did not in fact make uſe of it, to attend
the public worſhip of God : No ; but of perſons
that

the worſhip of God, where he was ſcarce wor-
ſhipped at all ; but in miſſions to thoſe places
in which the Goſpel was preached before, as
truly and faithfully, as it has been ſince ; if it

C 2   be

that have only changed, or were inclinable to
change, one mode of religiouſly ſerving God for
another ; and too often, there is reaſon to think,
without having thorowly inquired into matters
of this nature. Sometimes an account is given of
the " good morals of the people of their charge".
It might, I believe, with exact juſtice, be ſaid,
theſe were as good before, as ſince, their going to
Church. The plain truth is, had one half the
money been ſpared, for other uſes, that has been
expended upon New-England, thoſe places on the
American Continent which need it much more,
might have been better provided with the means
of ſalvation : Without all controverſie, the *poor
Indians* might have had more laborers ſent to them,
both in the capacity of miniſters and ſchool-maſters ;
and, it is probable, a large harveſt of ſouls would,
by this time, have been gathered in for Chriſt from
among them. It is generally thought here, if a
leſs proportion of this money was employed for the
ſupport of a party, and a far greater for carrying
the Goſpel to the numerous aboriginal natives,
who are totally ignorant of the true God, and of
his ſon Jeſus Chriſt, it would be as honorary to the
Society, and as " acceptable in the ſight of God
our Savior, who will have all men to be ſaved, and
to come to the knowledge of the truth".

I ſhall not think it unſeaſonable, or improper, to
ſubjoin here, We are eſpecially grieved that the
Society at home are not more zealous in their endeavours to propagate the Goſpel among the *Indian
natives,* as an effectual bar, a few years ſince, was
laid in the way of our exerting ourſelves to this
purpoſe, at leaſt by the inſtrumentality of a *Corpo-
ration* among our ſelves, The ſtory is briefly this.

Upon

be only fuppofed, that this can be done by minifters, not officiating according to the order of
the church of England. If one were to collect
their fentiments from their conduct, as reprefented in thefe abftracts, it muft be concluded,
that, with them, the propagation of the Gofpel,

Upon the conclufion of the late war, a general
fpirit was raifed in the people here to endeavour the
enlargement of the Redeemer's kingdom, by fend-
ing the Gofpel to the Tribes of Indians on our
weftern borders. They were defirous this affair
fhould be put under the management of fome a-
mong our felves of well-eftablifhed reputation for
wifdom, judgment and piety, and that they fhould
be *incorporated* by an act of the Government to
this end. Two thoufand pounds fterling were, in
a few days, fubfcribed, in Bofton only, upon this
condition. An incorporating act was accordingly
prepared, and paffed by the whole Legiflature of
this Province, and fent home for his Majefty's ap-
probation, without which it could not continue in
force. But it foon met with a negative, by means
whereof this whole money was loft, and as much
more we had good reafon to expect would have
been fubfcribed, befides the income of many hundred pounds fterling that had been devoted to the
fervice of the Indians. It is hoped, the accounts
we have had are not true, that the negative upon
this act was principally owing to the influence of
fome of the moft important members of the Society
for the propagation of the Gofpel. We are con-
tent not to have the honor of employing our own
money in endeavours to Gofpelife thefe Indians, if
the Society will heartily and thorowly engage in
it. We fhall rejoice to find, by their abftracts,
that needful Miffionaries are fent to them ; and far
from throwing any obftacles in their way, we
will do all in our power to encourage and help
them.

pel, and the eſtabliſhment of Epiſcopacy in the
Britiſh Colonies, were convertible terms. But
this in tranſitu.

Our complaint is, that the charge here
brought againſt theſe adventurers has really no
foundation for its ſupport. It is not pretend-
ed, that their endeavours to convert the natives were unmixed with human frailty. In
common with other good men, in other virtu-
ous undertakings, they had, no doubt, their
failings ; but not ſuch as may, with truth or
juſtice, be called *notorious* ones. And it is
really unkind, I may rather ſay cruelly hard,
to repreſent them to the world, as " becoming
themſelves infidels and barbarians", inſtead of
uſing their endeavours to " convert babarous
infidels". It is not eaſily conceivable, wherein
they could have exerted themſelves with more
zeal, or in more prudent ways, in endeavouring
to enlarge the borders of Chriſt's kingdom in
theſe " uttermoſt parts of the earth", by making the native barbarians the members of it.
It was out of their power to ſupport Miſſionaries among theſe heathen ; but, in other
ways, they laid themſelves out, to the utmoſt
of their power, as they had opportunity, for
their inſtruction in the " knowledge of God,
and Jeſus Chriſt, whom to know is life eternal".
And by their labors, eſpecially as encouraged
and aſſiſted by the London-Society, and more
privately, they ſo far effected the converſion

of them, as that numbers were prepared and difpofed to make an open profeffion of their faith in Jefus Chrift. The facred books of the old and new-teftament were, in their day, by the fkill and labor of the indefatigable ELIOT, * tranflated into the Indian-language, and difperfed among the natives for their in-ftruction in things pertaining to the kingdom
of

* He is to this day often fpoken of in that honorable ftyle, THE APOSTLE OF THE INDIANS. It was with great labor he made himfelf mafter of the *Indian language* ; and, as foon as he was thus ac-complifned, he preached to them in their own tongue, and in many of their villages : And, by the bleffing of God on his diligent endeavours, " many believed, and turned to the Lord". He foon had feveral companions, and afterwards fucceffors, who were faithful and zealous in inftructing thefe fava-ges in the Gofpel-method of falvation. Schools were erected among them, and fuch books put into their hands, in their native language, as their edi-fication called for. The confequence was, that, in feveral villages, *Indians* met together every Lord's day for the worfhip of God through Jefus Chrift, and Churches of them were gathered, who " walk-ed in the fear of theLord", and the religious obfer-vation of all Gofpel-ordinances. To the BIBLE, our Eliot added a verfion of the Pfalms in *Indian Metre*, which it was their practice to fing. This *Indian Bible* is the only one that was ever printed in this hemifphere of the univerfe ; as it is ex-preffed in the atteftation whence the above abftract is taken, which I fhall have occafion to mention in the next note. I fhall only add here, from Dr. Cotton Mather, in a fermon printed 1698, that " there were then in thisProvince more than thirty Indian affemblies, and more than thirty hundred chriftian Indians".

of God, and of Chriſt. And through his aſſi-
duous endeavours, with thoſe of the renowned
MAYHEW's, * and other worthies, a conſider-
able

* Mr. Thomas Mayhew, ſon of an excellent man of
this name, began, in another part of the Province,
the work of goſpeliſing the infidel-natives, ſo far
back as 1642. And this good work has been
carried on, by one and another of this name and fa-
mily, from that day to this. In 1657, many hundred *Indian* men and women were added to the
chriſtian Societies in this part of the Country, of
ſuch as might be ſaid to be " holy in their conver-
ſation", and that did not need, for knowledge, to
be taught " the firſt principles of the oracles of
God" ; beſides many hundreds of more ſuperficial
profeſſors. In the year 1689, the *Indian* church
under the care of Mr. John Mayhew, ſon of the
above Thomas, conſiſted of an hundred communi-
cants, walking according to the rule of the ſcrip-
tures. This is an extract from the Rev. Mr.
Thomas Prince's general account of the Engliſh
miniſters, who preſided at Martha's Vineyard.
The Rev. Mr. Experience Mayhew, ſon of the before mentioned John, and father of the late memorable Dr. Mayhew, a Gentleman of ſuch ſupe-
rior natural endowments, that he would, had he
been favoured with common advantages, have been
ranked among the firſt worthies of New-England ;
and who ſpent a life protracted ſeveral years beyond
eighty, in the ſervice of the Indians, publiſhed, in
the year 1727, an octato volume, entitled *Indian
Converts* ; in which he has given an account of the
lives of thirty *Indian* miniſters, and about eighty
Indian men, women, and young perſons, within
the limits only of Martha's Vineyard, an Iſland in
Maſſachuſett's-Province. And of theſe, as he was
a Gentleman of eſtabliſhed reputation for both
judgment and veracity, it may be charitably ſaid,
they were all real converts to the faith of Chriſt,
and

able number of churches, under the divine
blessing, were gathered, consisting of INDIAN
members, many of whom gave proof of the
reality of their conversion, by their walking in
the faith and order of the Gospel, so as to a-
dorn the doctrine of him, whom they now
called their only Savior and Lord. Some of
these churches have continued in succession
even to this day, with English, or Indian
Pastors at their head. * The above represen-
tation

and some of them in a distinguishing degree, clearly evidenced by their manner of life, which was
such as may make many English professors blush,
of whom it may be hoped, that they are christians in
truth, as well as name. In the *Attestation* to this
account, signed by eleven Boston ministers, some
of whom are now alive, it is said, " That they
" who may ignorantly and imperiously say, noth-
" ing has been done, may be confuted ; and that
" they, who are desirous to see something that has
" been done, may be entertained and gratified ;
" here is now exhibited a collection of examples,
" wherein the glorious grace of our great Redeemer
" has appeared to, and on, the INDIANS of New-
" England. It must not be imagined, these are all
" that could have been collected ; for all these are
" selected only from one Island".——It is said farther, " the author of this history, Mr. Experience
Mayhew, is a person of *incontestible veracity* :—We
again say, *his truth may be relied on, his fidelity is ir-
reproachable*".

* There are, at this day, within the Province of the
Massachusett's-Bay only, sixteen ministers, English
and Indian, statedly laboring, either as Pastors of
so many *Indian* churches, or as Preachers to assem-
blies of *Indians* that meet together for divine worship ;

tation is fo generally known here to contain the real truth, that it was greatly furprifing to many, to fee his Lordfhip fo impofed upon by fuch as were either grofly ignorant of what had been done by thefe adventurers, or wicked enough, in oppofition to their knowledge, to give him an account that was odioufly falfe and injurious.

His Lordfhip proceeds, " the pretences and " conditions were, that their defign was, and " that they fhould endeavour, the enlarge- " ment of commerce, and the propagation of " chriftian faith. The former they executed " with fincerity and zeal ; in the latter moft " notorioufly failed". He then adds in the immediately following paragraph, " Their " failure herein might well have been expect- " ed. Religion and traffic, their two profeffed " objects, are but ill yoke-fellows, being apt to " draw quite different ways : And men who " with defperate hardinefs invade unknown
D   " difficulties

fhip ; nine Englifh Lecturers, and feven ftated School-mafters, befides occafional ones : All which are under the care of Commiffioners here from the honorable Company for the propagation of the Gofpel in NEW-ENGLAND, and parts adjacant in AMERICA. The above account was handed to me from the records of thefe Commiffioners. There are, at the fettlement called Mafhpe, two hundred Indians, under the care of the Rev. Mr. Hawley, who know no God befides the ever-living Jehovah, and ftatedly pay worfhip to him through the one Mediator Jefus Chrift.

" difficulties and dangers in queft of gain;
" could not be fuppofed to be much concern-
" ed about fpiritual interefts. Religion is but
" an impediment in the way of avarice : Many
" things thereby prohibited; are deemed allow-
" able, and ftick clofe to traffic". Some of
the adventurers to this part of the world might
have the affair of commerce principally in their
view ; but, notwithftanding their " fincerity
and zeal", they foon found their miftake in
woful difappointment, and moftly returned
home. The fettlers of this part of America
were men of another turn. *Liberty to worfhip
God agreably to the dictates of confcience* was the
grand motive to their removal hither ; and the
enjoyment of this liberty at fo great a diftance
from *oppreffive power* was their fupport under
heavier tryals than can eafily be conceived of
by thofe who have never been in a wildernefs-
country. It might therefore be well expected
of fuch men, if of any in the world, that they
fhould not be guilty of " notorious failures" ;
as it is certain they were not. It is acknowledged, if " religion and traffic" had been their
" two profeffed objects", they would have
been " but ill yoke-fellows", for the reafons
his Lordfhip affigns. And may it not be faid,
for the like reafons, with equal propriety and
truth, that worldly dignity, riches and power,
conjoined with a profeffion and defign to ad-
vance

vance the intereſt of " a kingdom that is not
of this world", are as ill-matched companions.
Good may be, has been, and, I truſt, is now
done by thoſe, in whoſe view there was a regard to the honors and riches of this world, as
well as the promotion of Chriſtianity ; and the
ſame may be ſaid of others, in whoſe deſign
the objects united were religion and traffic. *

D 2   But

* An illuſtrious inſtance we have of this in Mr.
Thomas Mayhew, the firſt of this name in America.   He came over as a merchant to the Maſſachuſetts, in the early times of that plantation, and,
meeting with diſappointments in his buſineſs, he
procured, in 1641, a Grant or Patent of Sir Fer-
dinando Gorges, the Earl of Sterling's agent, for
Martha's Vineyard, Nantucket, & Eliſabeth Iſles, to
make an Engliſh ſettlement.   He was Governor as
well as Patentee of theſe Iſlands.   This led him, tho'
now about 55 years of age, to learn ſo much of the
language of the natives as was needful to under-
ſtand and diſcourſe with them.   And as he grew
in this acquirement, he was greatly helpful to his
ſon Thomas, now a preacher to them, in the pious
work of making them Chriſtians.   Upon the loſs
of this his excellent and only ſon in 1657, though
now in the 70th year of his age, an holy zeal for the
glory of God, and a moſt compaſſionate charity for
the ſouls of the periſhing Indians, kindle up in his
breaſt.   They raiſe him above all thoſe ceremonies,
forms and diſtinctions that lay in the way, and
which he accounted as nothing in competition with
their eternal ſalvation ; and he thereupon reſolves,
having no proſpect of a regular miniſter, to do his
utmoſt to carry on the good work that had been
begun among them, notwithſtanding all external
difficulties and diſcouragements.   He frequently
viſited, converſed with, and inſtructed this poor
                                        peop-

But thefe are cafes not very common ; as we
fhall foon fee, if we only look into paft hiftory.
By fo doing it will perhaps be found, that the
connection

people. He went once a week to fome of their
plantations. At fo advanced an age, he fet himfelf with unwearied diligence to perfect himfelf in
their difficult language ; and, tho' a Governor, yet
was not afhamed to become a preacher among
them. He ordinarily preached to fome of their
affemblies one day every week as long as he lived.
And his heart was fo exceedingly engaged in the
fervice, that he fpared no pains, nor fatigues at fo
great an age therein ; fometimes travelling on foot
nigh twenty miles through the woods to preach and
vifit, where there was no Englifh houfe near to
lodge at in his abfence from home. In a few
years time, with the affiftance of thofe religious
Indians who taught on the Lord's-day, he perfuaded
the natives on the weft-end of the Ifland to receive the Gofpel, who had many years been obfti-
nately refolved againft it ; fo that now the Indians
on the Ifles of Martha's Vineyard and Nantucket
might juftly bear the name of Chriftian. The
number of their adult, on both thefe Iflands, was
then about three thoufand. He went on labori-
oufly in this noble work of promoting the falvation
of the fouls of thefe Indians to the 93d year of his
age, when he died to the great lamentation both of
the Englifh and Indians.—When the incorporated
Society at home fhall fee fit, in their pious zeal for
the propagation of the Gofpel, to employ Miffionaries, as they might eafily do, among the *Indian
heathen* fettled all over this Continent, who fhall
exert themfelves with like refolute diligence and
fidelity, to" turn them from darknefs to light", in
oppofition to all the difficulties and hardfhips they
may be called to contend with, we will " highly
efteem them in love for their work's fake" ; and,
inftead of treating their names with reproach, we
will greatly " honor them in the Lord".

connection of honors, riches and power, with employments that are fpiritual, has been as fruitful an occafion of pride, haughtinefs, tam pering with Princes, and advifing and helping forward oppreffive tyranny over confcience, as the mixture of " traffic with religion" has ever been ofthofe deceitful fraudulent acts the latter prohibits.

It follows in the next words, "Commerce in-
" deed has been the occafion of communicating
" the knowledge of Chrift from nation to na-
" tion ; but perfons engaged therein have not
" been the communicators of it : Their bufi-
" nefs is of another fort. But this has been
" done by other men, detached from worldly
" affairs, and zealous and fkilful in divine
" knowledge ; who, taking the advantage of
" the intercourfe opened by them with other
" views, have preached the gofpel where it was
" before unknown. In this way our Planters
" have excelled, having given double occafion
" of propagating chriftianity among the na-
" tive heathen of thefe regions, and among
" themfelves alfo, who foon became heathen".

By the firft recited words in this paffage, the idea obvioufly and intentionally conveyed to the world is, that our Planters, being en-gaged in the bufinefs of traffic, might be the occafion of communicating the knowledge of
Chrift

Chriſt to the barbarians here, but that they were not themſelves the communicators of it. This was done by others, no doubt, the worthy miſſionaries from the Society at home; who, being detached from worldly affairs, and zealous and ſkilful in divine knowledge, took occaſion, from the intercourſe that had been opened with thoſe to whom the Goſpel was unknown, to preach it to them. So that it ſhould ſeem, theſe Miſſionaries, not the Planters, were the only perſons who had any hand in propagating Chriſtianity in theſe parts of the world. A goodly account truly! Nothing could have been ſaid more honorary either of the Society, or their Miſſionaries; and the glory reflected on them ſhines the brighter, as it is contraſted with the higheſt reproach that could be caſt on the Planters. The good people in England, who are unacquainted with the tranſactions in this new world, may be led, from the above repreſentation, into exalted apprehenſions of the pious endeavours both of the Society & their Miſſionaries. It is indeed well adapted to open their hearts and hands in contributions to carry on what they have ſo hopefully begun. But the unhappineſs is, heaven and earth are not more diſtant from each other, than this account is from the truth of the caſe; as We, who live here, do certainly know: For which reaſon, to ſay nothing more harſh, we are really aſtoniſhed.

By

By the latter ones, a great myſtery is opened. It always appeared to us an unaccounta-
ble thing, that the Society for propagating the
Goſpel in theſe foreign parts ſhould lay out
ſuch vaſt ſums of their money in ſupporting
Miſſionaries, eſpecially in places that were moſt
populous, and had, as we imagined, the leaſt
need of them ; but the difficulty is now un-
ravelled. We had given "DOUBLE OCCASION
of propagatingChriſtianity" ; that is,OCCASION
" AMONG OUR SELVES WHO SOON BECAME
HEATHEN", as well as " among the native
heathen of theſe regions". It is eaſily per-
ceivable, from what is here ſaid, that not only
hisLordſhip,but the incorporatedSociety before
whom he preached, unleſs their vote of thanks
was a meer compliment, look upon us as having made our ſelves " Heathen". And, if this
is our juſt character, proper occaſion was offer-
ed for the " propagation of Chriſtianity" a-
mong us ; and they have kindly pitied our
wretched caſe, and ſent a vaſt ſupply of help
to deliver us out of it. We are heartily ſorry
ſo very reſpectable a body of men ſhould en-
tertain ſuch a bad opinion of us. It can be
owing to one or other of theſe two cauſes only.
They either think, with ſome they have ſent
to us, that we have *no true miniſters, no accept-*
able worſhip, no valid adminiſtration of ſacra-
ments, and, in a word, *no religion of any value ;*
as

as our minifters have not had *the hands of fome Bifhop, in a lineal fucceffion from the Apoftles, impofed on them,* and our *religious fervices are performed conformably to the dictates of our confciences, and not that decent form which has been eftablifhed by the Government at home:* Or they have been led, by cruelly hard and notorioufly falfe reprefentations of us, to imagine, that we are become like to the native barbarous heathen themfelves; ignorant of God and our obligations to him; without any fenfe of religion, or practical regard to it; and given up to commit all uncleanefs and wickednefs with greedinefs. We would not think fo reproachfully either of his Lordfhip, or the Society, as to attribute the ill opinion they have conceived of us to the firft of thefe caufes: Nor fhall we be brought to it by any thing fhort of their plain affirmation in the cafe. We cannot therefore but fuppofe, that the Colonies have been fet before their view in an horribly abufive light, by fome fecret back-biters and revilers, through bigotry, prejudice, malice, intereft, or fome other luft of the flefh or mind.

His Lordfhip, in the next paragraph, having reflected blame upon the Government, in thefe times for the " defection" he had charged the Colonies with, and aggravated this blame by feveral weighty confiderations, expreffes himfelf, himself, pag. 10. in thefe words, "Now this "great evil, irreligion, might at firft have eafi- "ly been prevented growing in our Colonies; "but the fame evil, having been fuffered to "grow, hath been found fo hard to expel, "that now, after more than 60 years diligent "endeavour, it is very far from being era- "dicated". If by irreligion, the great evil fpoken of, is meant, the great impiety of ferv- ing God, without doing it after the mode of the eftablifhed Church at home, it is acknow- ledged, its "growth was not prevented at firft", if it might have been; and it has been "fuffer- ed to grow" ever fince, without interruption, until about the time of the Revolution in Eng- land, and fince then by the Society for the propa- gation of the Gofpel in foreign parts. And it is hoped, by at leaft twenty nine in thirty thro'- out New-England, that it will, inftead of be- ing eradicated, go on to grow, even to the end of time, notwithftanding all efforts that may be made to the contrary. If this be "irreli- gion", we are not afhamed to glory in it, tho' we fhould be accounted "fools for thus glory- ing"; nor are there wanting thofe here, who would efteem it "better to die than that any man", or body of men, "fhould make their glorying void" in this refpect. But if by the "growth of irreligion" his Lordfhip would be underftood to mean, the increafe of irreverence towards God, expreffed in an unbecoming

E   treatment

treatment of his name, perfections, and govern-
ing authority ; unrighteoufnefs towards men,
difcovered in the various ways of fraudulent
and cppreffive dealing ; and a difregard to the
great chriftian law of fobriety, made manifeft
by an indulgence to pride, luxury, extrava-
gance, uncleanefs, and thofe other lufts which
argue the want of due felf-government : I
fay, if this is what his Lordfhip means, by
" the growth of irreligion", he had no need to
have looked fo far for it as thefe diftant regions.
Unlefs the land which gave our fore-fathers
birth is greatly abufed, both by its own inhabitants, and others who have been there, it does
not come at all behind the Colonies in this
kind of growth, even heightned in malignity :
While yet, the whole body of *duly authorifed*
Clergymen, fuperior and inferior, have, if they
have done their duty, been diligently employing their time and pains, for more than 60
years many times told, to give check to it ;
and under the advantage too of that eftablifhed mode of performing divine fervice, which,
for a long time, was not in ufe here. And if
the abounding growth of iniquity could not
be prevented at home by the united force of
fo many regularly ordained minifters, high and
low, faithfully laboring to promote fo good a
defign, and in conformity to the prefcribed
order of the beft religious eftablifhment in the
world ; why fhould it be thought ftrange, if
there

there was the growth of like bad fruit in the
Colonies, which could not have been fo fully
favoured with the enjoyment of thefe advantages ?

What the true ftate of the fouthern Colonies
is, * I leave to be defcribed by thofe who are

E 2   better

---

* The prefent Arch-Bifhop of Canterbury, in his
fociety-fermon, preached, in 1741, when he was
Bifhop of Oxford, fpeaking of more of the Britifh
Colonies than one, fays, pag. 5. "There were fcarce
"any footfteps of Chriftianity left, beyond the
"meer name. No Teacher was known, no religious
"affembly held ; the Lord's-day diftinguifhed only
"by more general diffolutenefs ; the facrament of
"baptifm not adminiftred for near twenty years to-
"gether, nor that of the Lord's fupper for near fix-
"ty, among many thoufands of people, who did not
"deny the obligation of thefe duties, but lived
"notwithftanding in a ftupid neglect of them".
The more fouthern Colonies, it is fuppofed, are
here held forth to view ; as the defcription cannot,
with fo much as the fhadow of truth, be applied to
any other. And according to this reprefentation of
them, they were certainly fit objects of theSociety's
compaffionate regards ; efpecially as they were incorporated principally with a defign to extend their
care to fuch of the Plantations, whofe ftate was thus
deplorably fad. One would therefore naturally
think that, in proportion to their ability, and the
need of thefe places, they would have fent Miffionaries to perform the offices of religion among them.
And yet, if we look over their abft acts, we fhall
find, that their pious zeal has chiefly difcovered it
felf in miffions to other Colonies, where Teachers
abound, the worfhip of God on Lord's-days is generally and religioufly attended, and the facraments
of baptifm and the Lord's-fupper are as duly adminiftred

better acquainted with them than I can pretend to be. But, as to the more northern ones,
those particularly that are comprehended under

niftred as in England itfelf ; and this to the COM-
PARATIVE NEGLECT of the above defcribed places,
where there was fcarce any fenfe or appearance of
Chriftianity. What is here faid of the Society's
conduct is as true a fact, as that their abftracts relate the truth. It can, as I imagine, be accounted
for upon no principle but this, that they think they
fhall better anfwer the great defign of their incorporation by zealous endeavours to make converts from
Prefbyterianifm and Congregationalifm to Epifco-
pacy, than by propagating the gofpel in places that
have no Teacher, no public worfhip of God, no facraments, nor any footfteps of Chriftianity beyond
the meer name. If this is really their principle, it
is hoped they will not be averfe openly to avow it
in words, as they virtually do in their practice.

Thofe places are then fpoken of, pag. ibid. where the
ftate of things was " a little better", but ftill " lamentably bad". The more northern Colonies muft
be here intended. But why are they reprefented as
in circumftances lamentably bad ? For no reafon
that we know of here that could move the compaf-
fion of the Society, but this, that EPISCOPACY had
not got fuch ftrong footing here as they might defire. And however " affecting reprefentations might
be made" of our deplorable condition by " the inhabitants in thefe parts, by Governors, or principal
perfons of note", to ufe the language of the fermon,
a becoming regard to their honor as men of truth,
obliges us to fay, that their reprefentations muft refpect our ftate chiefly in this point of view, viz.
the non-pervalence of the Church among us. This,
I know, is, in the judgment of fome, the moft deplorable ftate a people can be in, however highly fa-
vored they may be with the means of grace, under
another mode of adminiftration, though more agre-
able to the purity and fimplicity of the gofpel.

der the name of New-England, it is acknowledged, they have too far departed from the simplicity, piety, and strict virtue of their fathers. There may be some infidels within these limits ; but their number, I believe, is very small. Those that are so came to us from abroad, or were corrupted by books wrote at home, and imported from thence. There are also to be found, in these parts, men of no conscience, dissolute in their manners, and accustomed to do evil ; ordering their conversation by fleshly wisdom, not by the grace of God. But this notwithstanding, I will be bold to say, true Christianity is not *more generally* better practised in any part of the world. There is not a town, or village, within these largely extended Colonies, (Rhode-Island Colony excepted) unless so lately settled as not to have had time for it, but is furnished with a house for the worship of God, and a minister set apart for the administration of Gospel-ordinances in it ; and, at these houses, there is every Lord's-day, and at other times also, a general resort of the people to attend on the public services of religion. I should not wrong the truth, should I say, that neither the Lord's-day, or his worship on that day, are more universally and devoutly regarded by any people on the earth. And as to the moral and christian virtues of faith in the being, perfections, revelations, and government of God, love to

him,

him, an holy fear of him, truft in his all-fufficiency, and fubjection to his will, however made known, whether in his word, or providential conduct, they are as *generally* poffeffed here, and thrown out into exercife upon proper occafions, as in any part of the known world. And it would be a wrong to thefe Colonies, fhould a contrary reprefentation be given of their character.

I fhall add here, whatever growth of vice there may be in thefe parts, it is as vifible in the cures of the Miffionaries from the Society, as where they are neither employed, or defired. And from hence it may be juftly concluded, as thefe Miffionaries, through the pious care of the Society, are as numerous here as any where on the American Continent, that this growth, in whatever degree it may prevail, is not owing to the want of *validly ordained minifters,* or *any fpecial mode of performing divine worfhip*; but to other caufes. What thefe are, it would be eafy, were it needful, to point out. They have operated, it may be, more powerfully in corrupting the nation at home, than its dependant Colonies. Whenever they are removed, religion, in unftained glory, will more univerfally take place both there and here; but not till then.

His Lordfhip fpeaks, a few pages onwards, of feveral things that obftruct the Society's endeavours

(39)

deavours to eradicate irreligion, the inveterate evil, so widely diffused over this vast tract of Country.

One is, to use his own words, pag. 19. "The "want of Seminaries in these parts, for the edu- "cation of persons to serve in the ministry of "the Gospel: A great disadvantage; so great, "that there is reason to apprehend, it may one "day undo all that the Society have been for "many years laboring to do". Had his Lord- ship thought it worth while to have more fully informed himself of the state of things in this part of the world, he would have found no reason for complaint upon this head. Seminaries for the education of persons to serve in the mi- nistry, or any other calling that would make a learned education proper, are, it may be, rather too numerous in the Colonies. They are more multiplied here, in proportion, than in Eng- land; though there may be no comparison be- tween their endowments. We have no less than six public Seminaries in North-America. Two of them, one at Virginia, the other at New-York, are Episcopal colleges; and a third, that at Philadelphia, has an Episcopal Clergy- man at its head. The other three are open to the sons of Church-men, in common with the sons of others; and they are admitted with the same freedom, and, I may add, without any previously required oaths, or subscriptions.
The

The moſt reſpectable of theſe Colleges for long
ſtanding, & endowments, is that at Cambridge
in the Maſſachuſetts-Province. *　There　is
　　　　　　　　　　　　　　　　　　ſcarce

*　This was the firſt College in the American world.
So far back as 1636, the Maſſachuſetts General Aſ-
ſembly gave £400 towards it's riſe. In the next
following year but one, the memorable *John Har-
vard* left, by his laſt will, one half of his eſtate to
carry on the ſame good deſign.　And this year,
1638, gives date to the foundation of this College.
It has ever ſince been known by the name of HAR-
VARD COLLEGE.　It was erected principally
for the Education of our ſons to ſerve in the work
of the Miniſtry, that, as Churches were multiplied,
there might be no want of ſutably qualified perſons
to take the paſtoral care of them.　And from hence
only they were ſupplied much the greater part of a
century ; and with more than a few of ſuch as made
a ſhining figure in their day.　Moſt of the beſt character in the Country for acquired accompliſhments,
who have ſerved either in Church or State, were
educated here, at leaſt until other Colleges were
erected.　It may be ſaid of this, without reflection,
that, in conſequence of donations, in former days
and more lately, from our own people, and from
abroad, it is the beſt endowed of any College on the
American Continent, though it may be below all
compariſon with the Colleges in Europe.　That
excellently good and catholic Gentleman, Mr.
THOMAS HOLLIS of London, ought always to be
mentioned with honor as one of its greateſt bene-
factors.　His liberal hand, beſides kindly benefiting
theCollege other ways, was ſtretched out to eſtab-
liſh two profeſſors in it ; the firſt, in 1722, for inſtruction in Divinity ; the other, in 1727, to teach
the Mathematicks and Philoſophy : Both which
eſtabliſhments have been greatly conducive to the
good education of the Students here.　His worthy
Nephew, and Heir, of the ſame name, and the like
　　　　　　　　　　　　　　　　　benevolent

scarce a Church-man, in this Province, of any figure, but has had one or more of his sons educated here; and it is from hence, that the Society at home have had, perhaps, the most of those they have employed in the New-England Colonies, which have been the greatest sharers in their pious care to propagate the Gospel. It may be farther said to the honor of this College, and in proof of their being actuated, not by a spirit of bigotry, but the noble spirit of true christian liberty, that, far from obliging their youths of Church-principles to join in public worship, where it is carried on after the Con-

F   gregational

benevolent Spirit, has, for many years, made this College the special object of his generous bounty; and it still keeps flowing in upon it, as from a never-failing fountain. No one can enter the College-Library-Chamber, but he will have full in his eye a large collection of very valuable and curiously chosen books, and be told in golden characters that they are his gift. I would yet say here, as this College has shewn so much candor and catholicism in its sentiments and conduct towards the Church of England; and as it has been so helpful to the Society at home in supplying them with most of their Missionaries for the northern Colonies, it would have been but a decent compliment, if it had been accounted worthy of some small part of the large sum lately collected throughout England for the benefit of Seminaries in these parts of the world. Such as were of Church-principles might have been educated for the *Indian-service* with as much freedom here as elsewhere; and, probably, as many might have gone from hence upon the noble design of carrying the Gospel to the barbarous natives.

gregational mode, they have excufed them
from it by a ftanding law made on purpofe :
Only, by the fame law, they are laid under obligations not to neglect divine fervice performed in the Epifcopal Church near the College ;
and in cafe of abfence, without fufficient reafon, they are fubjected to the fame fine the o-
ther youths are, if they groundlefly abfent
themfelves from the place where God is worfhipped in our way.   I fhall only add here, all
the churches of every other denomination receive conftantly a full fupply for the miniftry
from this and the other Seminaries ; and fo
might the church of England, if they pleafed.
There is no obftacle in the way, unlefs from
themfelves.   If therefore it has happened, that
" feveral Churches have ftood vacant, becaufe
none could be found to officiate in them", and
that the " fame want hath been an hinderance
to the proper work of the Society, and muft
needs prove an effectual bar to any farther con-
fiderable progrefs in it", as his Lordfhip fpeaks,
pag. 20. it muft be afcribed, not to the " want
of Seminaries" here, of which there are enough
already ; but to fome other caufe. The
Church-intereft can be in no danger from this
quarter.

Another difadvantage, attending the propagation of the Gofpel in thefe foreign parts, his
Lordfhip takes notice of, pag. 21. in the following

lowing words, " What encouragement have
" the inhabitants of thefe regions to qualify
" themfelves for holy orders, while, to obtain
" them, they lie under the neceffity of croffing
" an immenfe Ocean, with much inconveni-
" ence, danger and expence ; which thofe
" who come hither on that errand can but ill
" bear. And if they have the fortune to arrive
" fafe, being here without friends, and with-
" out acquaintance, they have the fad bufinefs
" to undergo, of prefenting themfelves un-
" known to perfons unknown, without any re-
" commendation or introduction, except cer-
" tain papers in their pocket. Are there not
" circumftances in this cafe, fufficient to deter
" every ordinary courage, and to dampt the
" moft adventurous fpirit".

It is acknowledged, it would be a great difcouragement to the fons of the Church from
qualifying themfelves for holy orders, and I
may fay to others alfo educated in the principles of the Country from taking them, if, in
order to obtain them, they muft crofs a wide
ocean at THEIR OWN EXPENCE. But this, I
prefume, is rarely, if ever the cafe. They are,
as we fuppofe upon good information, freed
from this difcouragement by being well provided for, if not by the Society in part at leaft,
by thofe who expect the benefit of their labors.
As for my felf, was I a candidate for holy or-

ders,

ders, I should esteem it a happy circumstance in the case, to have so fair an opportunity to visit the land of our fore-father's nativity. And I believe there are few but are encouraged by this very thing that is represented as a matter of so great discouragement. Their " being there without friends, and without acquaintance", is a difficulty made by imagination only. As they go from hence upon the nobly professed design of taking holy orders, that they may be validly commissioned to propagate the Gospel, it is impossible they should long want " friends or acquaintance", if it were only among the members of the Society, they are so numerous, and, at the same time, so earnestly engaged in promoting this pious design. It is true, the " business of presenting themselves unknown to those unknown friends would be sad", if they had no " recommendation except certain papers in their pocket". It is fit they should have these papers in readiness to be seen. Their moral qualifications can be known, at such a distance, only in this way. But it is as proper they should have knowledge in their heads, as papers in their pockets. And it is hoped, the Society send no Missionaries but such as are able to recommend themselves in the former, as well as the latter of these ways.

His Lordship now comes to the last and greatest inconvenience, " the want of Bishops in

in our Colonies". " This", says he, pag. 22.
" Besides other disadvantages attending it,
" appears, in particular, to be the fundamental
" cause of the want of native Ministers. The one
" removed; the other, it seems, would ceafe of
" courfe. For can it be imagined, could or-
" ders be had on the fame terms there as elfe-
" where, that a number of the natives suffici-
" ent for the fervice of the Church, would
" not offer themfelves in thofe, as they do, in
" all other parts of Chriftendom".

The want of " native minifters", if this is
really the cafe, is not, I believe, owing to any
of the caufes his Lordfhip has mentioned, not
excepting that of there being " no Bifhops in
the Colonies". If I may fpeak here with the
fame freedom that I think, I would fay, there
is, in one refpect, an obvious difference between
our people, and thofe who profefs themfelves
Church-men. The former generally fend their
fons to one or other of our Colleges with a view
to their being educated for the miniftry ; this
is rarely done by the latter. Should any afk
the reafon of this ;—it muft be plainly faid, our
Churches are numerous for a new Country,
many of them large, and well capable of providing for their minifters ; and, by a fwift increafe of inhabitants and new-fettlements, they
are daily growing both in number and ability
to fupport their Clergy. There is herefrom

the

the profpect of a tolerable provifion for our fons, if educated to ferve in the miniftry. Whereas, there are very few Epifcopal churches that " ftand upon their own legs";—and by far the greater part of the other are fmall in num- ber, weak in ability, and infufficient to main- tain their own miniftry, unlefs affifted by the Society at home. It is this that difcourages the Church-people from bringing up their fons for Clergymen. They chufe rather to provide for them fome other way. And as to profelytes from us, the temptation ordinarily is fo fmall, that few are overcome by it until they have found there was little or no profpect of their being employed to greater advantage. No one need now be at a lofs to affign the true caufe of the "; want of native minifters".

But if Bifhops fhould be fent to the Colonies, the people would generally turn Church-men ;-- the Ecclefiaftical ftate of things would foon be inverted ;—Epifcoparians would quickly ex- ceed the other denominations of Chriftians, as much as they now exceed them.

This, without all doubt, is the grand point aimed at ; and there may be fome, both at home and here, who really think all this would fpeedily come into event. But thofe who are beft acquainted with the genius, temper and principles of the Colonifts, at leaft in thofe parts where they are moft numerous, have not the

leaft

leaft motion of fear excited in them from the
profpect of any fuch effect of the miſion of
Biſhops. They are rather concerned, leaſt it
ſhould be the occaſion of hurtful confequences
both to them and us. Such confequences
would certainly be the effect, if theſe Biſhops
ſhould make uſe of their SUPERIORITY, as
moſt probably they would, fooner or later, to
influence our great men here, and much greater ones at home, to project, and endeavour to
carry into execution, meaſures to force the
growth of the Church. It may be relied on,
our people would not be eaſy, if reſtained in
the exerciſe of that " liberty wherewith Chriſt
has made them free" ; yea, they would ha-
zard every thing dear to them, their eſtates,
their very lives, rather than ſuffer their necks
to be put under that yoke of bondage, which
was fo ſadly galling to their fathers, and occa-
ſioned their retreat into this diſtant land, that
they might enjoy the freedom of men and
chriſtians.

His Lordſhip ſpeaks, pag. ibid. of the want
of Biſhops, as the " more heavily lamentable";
becauſe " all fects of Proteſtant chriſtians at
home, and all fave one (meaning the Church
of England) throughout the Colonies, have
the full enjoyment of their religion".

A ſtranger to the Colonies would be apt to
think, from this cauſe of lamentation, that the
Epiſcopal

Epifcopal Churches here, inftead of enjoying the liberty that is common to the other denominations of chriftians, were in a ftate of religious oppreffion : Whereas the real truth is, not the leaft reftraint is laid upon their chriftian liberty. They worfhip God when, where, and how they pleafe, without hindrance or moleftation : Yea, they are diftinguifhed from all other denominations in this refpeft, that they are the only objects of the pious charitable help of the richeft Society in all England incorporated upon a religious defign. And they are befides, within the Maffachufetts Province, [how it is in the other Colonies I know not] favoured by a ftanding law that excufes them from paying towards the fupport of any minifters but their own.

But they have " no Bifhops". Very true ; and they have no juft reafon for complaint upon this head. For, let it be confidered,

Throughout an extent of territory more than 500 miles in length, comprehending feven Provinces, the four New-England ones, and thofe of New-York, the Jerfies, and Penfylvania ; I fay, throughout thefe largely extended Provinces, fo well inhabited that they contain more than a million of fouls, there are not, by the beft information I can get, more than eight or nine Epifcopal churches that fupport themfelves. All the reft, to the amount of about fixty, more or lefs, chiefly made up of converts from the other denominations

tions of Chriftians, are fo far upheld in their exiftence by the Society at home, at the expence
of not lefs than fome thoufands fterling per an-
num, that, fhould this be withdrawn, they would
foon fink away for want of needed affiftance.
Inftead now of being contented with the receipt
of fo much pious charity, they think it hard,
and complain of it as a moft lamentable thing,
that as many thoufands fterling more are not
annually laid out for the maintainance of Bifhops
among them. Is this reafonable ? Would
Church-men themfelves think it fo in regard of
other denominations of chriftians befides themfelves ? Should any of thefe denominations, in
like circumftances, make the like complaints, in-
fifting that they were not fuffered " fully to enjoy their religion", none, it may be, would treat
their complaints with more contempt, than thofe
who are themfelves fo loud in making them.
And yet, I know not, in regard of real merit,
but other denominations would have as good a
right to complain, as thofe who profefs themfelves members of the Church of England.   For
they are the defcendants from anceftors, who
fubdued & cultivated this rude wildernefs, amidft
a thoufand difficulties & hazards, fo as to make it
the pleafant fruitful land we now behold it ; hereby adding to the extent, ftrength and glory of
the Britifh Crown : Nor has that facred Majefty
who wears it more loyal fubjects, even in England itfelf : And as they are far more numerous

than

than the Epifcoparians, they are in proportiori more able, and I am fure they would be as willing; to exert themfelves, if called to it, at the peril of their lives, in defence of his Perfon and Dominions.

His Lordfhip farther mentions it as an aggravating circumftance attending the want of Bifhops, that " even the Romifh fuperftition within a Province lately added to the Britifh Dominions; is compleatly allowed in all points ; it hath Bifhops and Seminaries".

It is prefumed, if Bifhops are allowed in that Province,they are provided for by eftablifhments within itfelf,when the inhabitants were fubjects of the King of France ; not at the expence of the Britifh Crown or Nation, as it muft be if Bifhops are fent to fuper-intend theEpifcopal churches in the Colonies ; which makes a wide difference betwixt the two cafes. But be this as it may, the fact itfelf may be efteemed certain, as it is affirmed by his Lordfhip, whofe fituation leaves no room to fufpect a miftake in a matter of this nature. And an aftonifhing one it is to us in thefe parts of the world ! THE ROMISH SUPERSTITION COMPLEATLY ALLOWED IN ALL POINTS ! What more furprifing ! What more oppofite to one of the great ends propofed by King William IIId, in incorporating the Society for the propagation of the Gofpel in thefe foreign parts! What could more powerfully obftruct one main
branch

branch of their proper bufinefs, the prevention, or extirpation, of Popery in the Colonies! We may reafonably fuppofe, his Lordfhip, and the whole incorporated body of which he is a member, are ftrongly affected with grief at this COMPLEAT ALLOWANCE ; and that they will unite in all proper remonftrances upon fo important an occafion. How far articles of capitulation may have made way for fuch an *allowance,* I pretend not to judge ; but if, in virtue of any of them, it was made neceffary, a confent to them was highly impolitic, and may be of dangerous confequence to the Britifh intereft, more efpecially in that part of America.

His Lordfhip concludes what he had to fay upon the head of Bifhops with thefe words, pag. 25. " This point obtained, [the miffion of Bifhops to the Colonies] the American Church will foon go out of its infant ftate ; be able to ftand upon its own legs ; and without foreign help fupport and fpread itfelf. THEN THE BUSINESS OF THIS SOCIETY WILL HAVE BEEN BROUGHT TO THE HAPPY ISSUE INTENDED."

The conduct of the Society has, for many years, given us reafon to fufpect their MAIN VIEW was to EPISCOPISE the Colonies ; but we were never before, that 1 know of, told fo in direct terms. His Lordfhip, in the prefence of theSociety themfelves, has not only fpecified,

their

their BUSINESS, but in plain words declared,
that it will be brought to its INTENDED HAP-
PY ISSUE, if they may "but have Bishops, and
the Church go out of its infant state so as to
support and spread itself". We are firmly per-
suaded, if their proper business is here pointed
out, and they prosecute it with the greatest vi-
gor, the " happy issue they intend" will never
take place, according to their desire, at least in
the New-England Colonies. These, for scores
of years, have been the special object of their sol-
licitous care ; and may have cost them, from first
to last, more a great deal than thirty thousand
pounds sterling. And what has been the effect ?
There has gradually been the rise of about thirty
three Episcopal churches, by far the greater part
of which are so small in number, and to this day
so insufficient for their own support, that, should
the Society's pious charity towards them be dif-
continued, there would be no probable hope of
their long continuance in being : Whereas, the
Congregational and Presbyterian churches only,
without any charitable help from abroad, and in
opposition to all efforts to prevent it, have in-
creased to the number of 550 ; and they go on
increasing, as much in proportion beyond the E-
piscopal churches as they exceed them in number
and ability. Why then should theSociety expect
" the happy issue they intend" ? There is no rea-
sonable room for hope in the case : Especially, if
it be remembered, that we, in these parts, not
only

only know the ERRAND of our fore-fathers into this Country, but have been well indoctrinated in the PRINCIPLES OF CHRISTIAN LIBERTY. " Old grudges and jealoufies" are no " obftacles" in the way of our going over to the Church ; and as to " obfolete piques & groundlefs fears", they are as fully "extinguifhed" here as in "England". We prefer our own mode of worfhip and difcipline to that of the Englifh church ; and we do it upon principle, as really believing that it comes nearer to the purity and fimplicity of Gofpel-direction. And as thefe are the generally prevailing fentiments inNew-England, and their conduct has all along been generally conformable hereto, we have no fearful apprehenfions of a departure herefrom ; but are rather fully perfuaded, they will ftand faft to their principles, and clofely adhere to that mode of worfhip which has hitherto been in ufe among them, whatever attempts may be made to turn them afide.

You fee, Sir, I have endeavoured to comply with your defire. I hope your expectations will not be difappointed. Poffibly, your view may be to publifh thefe remarks. As to this, you may do as you pleafe. No one is better able to judge of the propriety or truth of the facts above related ; and I may depend, if they will not bear your fcrutiny, they will have your perufal only.

I am, with great Refpect,

Bofton, Dec. 10. 1767.

Your obliged, obedient, and humble Servant,

CHARLES CHAUNCY.

P. S.

AS you faid nothing to me of the Society-fermon, preached by Dr. Warburton, Lord Bifhop of Gloucefter, in 1766, I conclude you had not feen it. While I was finifhing the foregoing remarks, his Lordfhip's third vol. of fermons on various occafions, in which this was contained, was put into my hands. It will not, I believe, be unacceptable, if I tranfcribe two or three paffages in it for your perufal.

Pag. 65. " But though the zeal of the firftColonifts " (rekindled by this violent remove to the otherHemi- " fphere) kept religion alive and active, yet their. " poverty difabled them from fupplying fuel to the " vital flame ; I mean, provifion for A PREACHING " MINISTRY. Infomuch, that without the kindly " affiftance of their Mother-Country, this new chri- " ftian Common-wealth had been, as the Roman " hiftorian expreffes it of the imperial City in it's " cradle, Res unius Ætatis. Againft this danger, " a timely aid was to be provided. And the Foun- " ders of our Society", &c. We doubt not his Lord- fhip's thorow acquaintance with the hiftory of other more important Countries, even from their firft rife ; but the ftory of this has certainly been below his notice. Otherwife, he would have known, that fome of the " firft Colonifts" were men of ample fortunes for that day.—He would have known alfo, if it was their unhappinefs to be poor, that, notwithftanding their poverty, they did in fact " fupply fuel to the vital flame", that is, make provifion for a PREACHING MINISTRY ; infomuch, that, " without any kindly affiftance of their Mother-Country", they had a fufficiency of Minifters for the performance of the public offices of religion, wherever they extended their fettlements.

tlements. He would have known farther, that there, had been nearly the revolution of an age, if a century may be fo called, and an increafe of Churches to fome hundreds, with Paftors at the head of them, before the exiftence of that incorporated body which was to fupply a *preaching Miniftry*, without which religion could not be kept alive. And He would have known moreover, that, fince the incorporation of this Society, the growth of Churches, and their fupply with Minifters, at leaft in the New-England Colonies, has been much more than ten times greater without any help from them, than where they have afforded it at an immenfe expence.

Pag. 67. " Here then we might well leave thefe " contentious people to themfelves, did not a mifer- " able circumftance ftill call for our rejected charity : " I mean, the fpreading GENTILISM in the Colonies " themfelves. Not a brutal ignorance of God, as among the Savage natives ; but a BLASPHEMOUS CONTEMPT of his holy difpenfations, among our *Philofophic Colonifts*". With what truth, or juftice, this reproach is caft upon the Colonies may be feen in the foregoing remarks. Only it may be faid here, if there are any " Philofophic Colonifts" who " blaf- pheoufly contemn God's holy difpenfations", they are not confined to the defcendants from " Fanatics" ; but may as well be looked for in the Church, that has been the fpecial object of the Society's care ; they themfelves being judges.

It follows in the next words, " The origine of " which folly was, however, no more than this.—— " The rich product of the Plantations foon fupplied " the Colonifts with all the conveniences of life. " And men are no fooner at eafe, than they are ready
" addreffed

" addreſſed to pleaſure. So that the ſecond venture
" of our Coloniſts was for *the luxuries of ſocial life :*
"Among which the commodity called FREE-THINK-
" ING was carefully conſigned to them, as that which
" gave a reliſh and ſeaſoning to all the reſt.—Thus
" it came to paſs, that the VERY PEOPLE, whoſe
" fathers were driven for conſcience-ſake into the
" *waſte and howling wilderneſs,* is now AS READY TO
' LAUGH AT THAT BIBLE, the moſt precious relict
" of their ruined fortunes, as at their ruffs and collar-
" bands". Surely, his Lordſhip would not have ſaid
this, had it not been told him by ſome, profeſſing an
acquaintance with the poſterity of thoſe, who were
driven into this wilderneſs. But be they who they
may, " the truth was not in them".—They could
not more baſely or falſely have ſpoken evil of them.

I ſhall only add, the reproachful light in which the
Colonies are placed, more eſpecially in the two laſt
Society-ſermons, may poſſibly tend to move the com-
paſſion of ſerious good people at home, and enlarge
the exerciſe of their pious charity towards us ; but
the growth of the Church here, the great thing in
view, will rather ſuffer than gain by it. Were theſe,
and a few more ſermons breathing the ſame Spirit, to
be reprinted and diſperſed among the Colonists, it
would, I am perſuaded, diſſerve the Church much
more, than the miſſion of as many Biſhops as could
be wiſhed, would ſerve it.

Your's as above,

C. C.

www.ingramcontent.com/pod-product-compliance
Lightning Source LLC
Chambersburg PA
CBHW031756090426
42739CB00008B/1034